DIFFERENTIATING BETWEEN MARKETING STRATEGY AND OTHER STRATEGIES.

A COMPREHENSIVE BREAKDOWN DIFFERENTIATNG MARKETING STRATEGY FROM OTHER STRATEGIES

INTRODUCTION

Many small to medium sized businesses face a common struggle; a balancing act of plans, strategies, departments and decisions. All of the elements are present, all of the gears in working condition, but business isn't exactly booming at the pace it had anticipated or forecasted for. What exactly does this growth and sustainability require? In a turbulent economy teeming with congested airwaves and aggressive business practices, it's about standing out from the crowd. And surprisingly, your marketing strategy has a lot more to do with it than you might realize. Conflicted business owners can overcome the masses and draw the customers that are right for their product by executing a stellar marketing strategy, not by yelling louder than their competitors or using neon banners on their storefront (or banner ads on your website). My point is, you don't have to be throwing yourself out there with a bunch of noise all the time. What you need to do is paint a vision for your business, your employees, and your customers. Make promises that nobody but you can keep, and then blow them away with your admirable businesses practices and superhuman skills. Take a moment to consider this: marketing strategy is the single most important factor in determining the prosperity or deterioration of a business. That's a pretty substantial claim and I'm willing to prove its legitimacy. Marketing strategy distributes itself throughout all the facets of a business, whether intended by its creator or not. This is possible because the strategy is created and defined by the overall objectives of a specific business, and integrates these objectives with a company's unique vision and mission. Put simply, every level of a business should be oozing marketing strategy. Really! Marketing Strategy Does it seem far-fetched? Let's examine the relationship between marketing strategy and four key aspects of any business: market research, the marketing plan, corporate identity, and the economy. First, let's get the formalities out of the way and set forth a definitive explanation of what marketing strategy actually is. After scouring several websites for the official definition, I settled on a less-official but more effective description of marketing strategy: Marketing Strategy: A strategy that integrates an organization's marketing goals into a cohesive whole. Ideally drawn from market research, it focuses on the ideal product mix to achieve maximum profit potential. The marketing strategy is set out in a marketing plan. While your marketing strategy is, essentially, a document; its purpose is far more load bearing. Included in the strategy should be your mission statement and business goals, an exhaustive list of your products and services, a characterization or description of your target clients, and a clear definition of how you integrate into the competitive landscape of your industry.

MARKETING STRATEGY V.

MARKET RESEARCH

This relationship establishes an order of operations: the first phase in any marketing or branding initiative is research. No matter the scope of your research, whether it is a broad canvassing of your current client list or unveiling specific, detailed findings about your target market, the outcome will have a direct effect on your marketing strategy. It's imperative to find out everything about whom you are trying to reach. What generation are they in? How big are their families? Where do they live, eat, and hang out? How do they spend their free time and money? All of this information will influence and alter your marketing strategy. Research alone will not benefit your business without a solid marketing strategy. Often, business owners narrowly define market research as the collection and organization of data for business purposes. And while that is technically an accurate definition, the emphasis lies not on the process of research itself, but the impact it commands on future decisions regarding all levels of a company. Every business decision presents different, unique needs for information, and this information then shapes a suitable and applicable marketing strategy. Research can be a grueling, confusing, and tedious process. From establishing or cleaning out a database to creating surveys and conducting interviews, you can receive a lot of information about your clients and potential clients and wonder what to do next. Before beginning to formulate a strategy, the information and data collected must be organized, processed, analyzed, and stored. Rest assured, with a little creativity and a lot of effort, this will all be molded into a structured, effective, and easily adaptable marketing strategy. Furthermore, continuous and updated research will ensure your strategy is a current and relevant reflection of your target market, marketing goals, and future business endeavors.

MARKETING STRATEGY V. MARKETING PLAN

In this relationship, the marketing strategy is essentially a guide to judge the performance and efficiency of a specific marketing plan. In simple terms, a marketing strategy is a summary of what you offer and how you are positioned in the market (in relation to competitors' products and services), and your marketing plan is an organized list of actions that you will enforce to achieve the goals outlined in your strategy. The plan will encompass the steps to a real-life application of a marketing strategy, bringing life Marketing Strategy and Planning: The Road Map to your mission and vision. It's your time to show and sell your products and services so that your target market can experience them in the presence that you truly imagined. Often, businesses lack a balance of creative personality and logic personality. While a business owner might have the creativity to dream up a stellar product, business model, and brand, they may lack the entrepreneurship and discipline to bring it all to life through research, planning and execution.

MARKETING STRATEGY V. CORPORATE STRATEGY

Identity It's no surprise that some of the most successful and recognizable companies in the world are those who establish distinguished, one-of-a-kind cultures that permeate through every channel of a business and reach customers on a human level. The culture of a corporation, its psychology, attitude, approaches to business, values and beliefs, lays the groundwork for a unique and compelling corporate identity. There is a powerful and undeniable connection between the health of these companies and the identities that their culture has provided. These companies have discovered the delicate balance between a brand and a strategy, and how this symbiotic connection encourages visibility and growth. The relationship is simple: the marketing strategy represents where a company wants to go, and the culture determines how (and sometimes if) it will get there. Think of a corporate identity - the style, words, images, and colors - as the personification of your marketing strategy. The corporate identity is extended and applied in every phase of the marketing strategy, and plays a stylistic role in its execution. Let's look at an example. Starbucks, until recently, didn't really have a marketing or advertising budget, per se. Starbucks started advertising in the New York Times and on TV in 2009, and very gingerly at that. Once a week it would print full-page ads in the Times, and on select channels it would air brief, lighthearted commercials. Prior to, the company was able to very successfully promote itself and its products through word of mouth and slapping the 25-year-old logo on every cup its baristas cranked out, proving that even something as simple as a logo can deeply resonate with consumers. But it was the Starbucks' identity that its millions of customers were happily waiting fifteen minutes in line for. The infamous Starbucks cup rapidly became associated with wealth, leisure, high standards, and urbanites. From college freshman to corporate CEO's, people couldn't get enough. Starbucks enforced its marketing strategy through clever, catchy campaigns, a genuine and human "front line" at the store level, and for the most part, acknowledging any mistakes or shortfalls that it might've run into. All of these actions are traits, portraying a deeply rooted culture that is exuded from top to bottom of the Starbucks hierarchy. And, love them or hate them, there's no denying their great success, even in a strained economy.

MARKETING STRATEGY V.

THE ECONOMY

The economy is an incredibly sensitive subject around the globe. What we've also noticed is that a lot of companies and business owners are using a depressed economic state as a reason (and in some cases, an excuse) for the shortcomings in their business. For example, a big trend recently has been layoffs. Larger corporations are using weak economies as a reason to purge its staff and cut positions, when it knows just as well that that's exactly the opposite of what needs to happen. Or does it? It's become hard to tell. Is surviving a "depression" really as simple as, say, reassessing your marketing strategy? While an unstable economy is troubling, risky, and unpredictable, it's also an excellent test of the flexibility of your marketing strategy. Your strategy isn't set in stone...the whole purpose of designing a strategy in the first place is for smooth navigation through any given circumstance, whether good or bad. Unfortunately, many CEOs and CFOs target their marketing departments first in lean times, while the reality is that it should be investing in these areas so that its marketing managers can adjust their strategy to survive-maybe even prosper, through tough times. An excerpt from the blog of R. Bruer, the owner and head of a strategic communications firm in Portland, Oregon, lays it all out: "Most businesses treat marketing as a discretionary expense, making it an easy target for budget cutters. It's as if marketing is a luxury afforded only when times are flush. Less customer demand, less we can afford marketing, or so conventional thinking goes. But really, can we ever afford not to market? It's natural to want to preserve cash during a downturn. I was an employer for nearly 14 years, so I'm sympathetic. But the tendency is to make deep cuts in marketing when sales head south. Companies often start by reducing or eliminating outside expenses, such as advertising, events, sponsorships, research. And when that's not enough, they lay off marketing employees, sometimes the entire department. The net effect of gutting marketing is to stifle generation of customer awareness,

demand and retention just when these

things are needed most. It's a penny-

wise, pound-foolish decision."

MARKETING STRATEGY

AND PLANNING

The Road Map Your Marketing Strategy While marketing strategy isn't tangible, its role in business is just as dire as the product or service being offered. Its contribution bears significance through every phase of a business plan, from conception to execution and far beyond these four aspects of research, planning, identity and economy. Marketing strategy will continue to fold itself into business plans as long as it is created and executed properly. Research on your industry and competitors will enable you to develop and formulate a proper, pliable strategy. From here, your marketing plan will act as a guide that will bring your strategy to life, attaining and exceeding the goals outlined, all while establishing your corporate culture and identity. Remember, the culture piece works two ways. Your culture helps to form the strategy, and following that strategy will reinforce your culture. Lastly, your strategy must be both strong and flexible enough to withstand the most difficult or unpredictable of circumstances, such as an economic depression, new trends or competitors in your industry. Strategy is a small piece of a much larger picture. It can all be overwhelming at times, sure, but it's part of the adventure. With dedication, organization, and a champion marketing team the pieces will come together with ease, allowing for the truly awesome personality of your business to shine, and profits to follow shortly thereafter

MARKETING STRATEGY VS TACTICS

What's the difference between strategy vs. tactics?

Strategy dictates the marketing activity needed to achieve your business goals and vision, whereas tactics, the 'detail of the strategy', answer how exactly that will happen.

Strategy defines competitive advantage

Looking at strategy through the lens of how precisely you can compete against competitors is a good way of distinguishing between strategy and tactics. If it fits your mindset, you can think of it as your 'rules of engagement' in a battle or war.

Sun-Tsu was certainly the first to write about this and Sun-Tsu's strategic thinking can be readily applied to marketing strategy, his well-known, but likely apocryphal quote illustrates this well:

"Strategy without tactics is the slowest route to victory. Tactics without strategy is the noise before defeat".

Strategy defines top-level resource allocation

Every business has limited resources of budget, people, and time at their disposal in the same way a general does. So, an essential part of the strategy is deploying these resources to drive the biggest impact.

I like the technique of informing strategy by deciding what you WON'T invest in addition to deciding where you will focus. In this classic Harvard Business Review paper, it's suggested that many strategies fail because they are not strategies at all, instead, they are simply aspirations...

"One major reason for the lack of action is that "new strategies" are often not strategies at all. A real strategy involves a clear set of choices that define what the firm is going to do and what it's not going to do".

MARKETING STRATEGY VS. SALES STRATEGY

Marketing and sales are usually the two major drivers of any business. Without a strategy for each, there is no company growth.

A marketing strategy is how you will reach your target audience, while a sales strategy is how you will convert them to customers. A marketing strategy sets the direction for how you will find and engage with prospective customers so you can promote your core message and build interest in the brand. Conversely, a sales strategy describes how you will sell to that target audience and turn prospects into buyers.

Both marketing and sales are essential parts of the customer journey — from awareness to purchase. Teams must align on these two strategies, and that means understanding both convergence and divergence points.

Now, sales is not something I write about frequently. (And when I have, my point of view has been different than most.)

We have never had a sales team at Aha! And no one has ever earned a penny of commission. Instead, we hire product and marketing experts who engage customers in a consultative way, freely sharing best practices and product knowledge.

Of course, I understand that our approach is unique. And I have lived both sides, working with enterprise companies that employ a traditional sales strategy. So, I want to share some insight that I have learned over the years.

Here are the key differences between the sales strategy and the marketing strategy:

Why

The purpose of a marketing strategy is to capture and define marketing goals. This includes plans for how you will promote your product or service to reach the right customers, as well as for how you will achieve (and maintain) a competitive advantage in the market. A goal-first marketing strategy aligns the team around what you want to achieve — so you can identify the right programs and advertising campaigns to invest in.

The purpose of a sales strategy is to create the most effective path for turning interested prospects into paying customers. It focuses on how you will work directly with the people who are most likely to make a purchase and how you will help them choose to start paying for your product or service. A sales strategy may also address tactics for turning one-time customers into repeat buyers or referral sources.

What

The marketing strategy usually contains the following:

Company vision and goals

Value proposition

SWOT Analysis

Marketing Goals

Initiatives

Brand essence

Positioning

Customers Personas

Competitive landscape

The sales strategy usually contains the following:

Forecasting

Prospecting

Lead tracking

Channel support

Customer meetings

Discounting strategies

Opportunity tracking

Who

The marketing strategy is generally set by the CMO or VP of marketing, but various members of the marketing team help drive it. This is because the marketing team works directly with groups that influence customers — such as product, product marketing, support, and sales.

The sales strategy is generally set by the VP of sales or the chief revenue officer. It is then implemented by sales representatives and new business managers. Rather than interact with the entire audience that marketing targets, salespeople usually focus on a subset. So, the sales team may speak to folks individually or interact with a few qualified leads at a time.

When

A marketing strategy is long-term and ongoing. Since it can help inform the sales strategy, it should be created first. You should also periodically revisit your marketing strategy to make adjustments based on any changes to your budgets, tools, or team.

A sales strategy is typically short-term. Because it builds upon the marketing strategy, a sales strategy is typically formulated later. You may need to make occasional adjustments to this strategy, depending on whether the sales team is hitting or missing sales goals.

How

A successful marketing strategy requires constant communication. Everyone on the team needs to understand how the marketing strategy will help to accomplish larger company goals. There should also be a focus on promoting the brand promise to customers, as well as using tools like business models, demographic research, and competitive analysis.

A successful sales strategy builds upon the work done by the marketing team by homing in on specific prospects who are most likely to buy. This is usually true unless the sales team drives a significant percentage of its own opportunities. Direct sales organizations are busy following leads, making discovery calls, qualifying prospects, pitching the product or service, building relationships, and converting prospects to customers.

Marketing and sales strategies work in tandem to connect with customers and grow the business.

MARKETING STRATEGY VS COMMUNICATION STRATEGY

Clients frequently ask me to describe the difference between marketing and communications. Many confuse the two because, quite frankly, it is confusing. However, understanding the difference will help your business in creating a strong brand, boosting your bottom line and protecting your reputation. To help clear things up, here are a few fundamental distinctions.

The customer is king in marketing

Marketing is a vital component of your overall business plan with the customer or client as the focus of marketing activities. Many marketing plans include competitive analysis, sales forecasts, target market research and industry trends, as well as identify specific activities such as communications to reach existing and new customers. If you are a nonprofit organization, the focus of your marketing plan will likely be your financial supporters, both individuals and institutions.

Communications are the storyteller

Communication plans advance marketing efforts by developing compelling messaging related to your services or products. While communication plans are a tactic within the marketing plan, it too should be strategic. You will likely need to conduct customer interviews and implement communication surveys to develop the right messages that resonate with your audience.

In addition to outlining the story and messaging, communication plans identify the best ways to tell the story, i.e., media, advertising, social media, newsletters or whitepapers.

What about marketing communications?

A sophisticated suite of marketing communications shares your story and influences customers to buy a service or product. Marketing communications include direct mail campaigns, brochures, website content and presentations. Thanks to our shortened attention spans and our limited time, it is crucial to incorporate visuals into your marketing communications. An infographic, photograph or short video can tell a compelling product or service story instantaneously.

Communications cast a wider net

While marketing plans are specific for customers or clients, communication plans may cast a wider net by creating messaging for other stakeholders including employees, neighbors, public and government officials as these audiences could play a significant role in the success of your marketing endeavors. For example, with a new product coming to market in the U.S., one petrochemical company developed a sophisticated global marketing effort. Also, a communication effort was built and implemented locally to ensure the community was well informed of the production site's activities, as the plant was ramping up. Communication tactics and outreach included town halls, newsletters and public tours of the site. While these community-stakeholders aren't direct customers to the petrochemical company, they could undoubtedly delay production efforts if there were serious concerns from the community.

In summary, while a marketing plan outlines target markets to penetrate based on favorable economic trends, the communications plan develops the product or service story to customers and other stakeholders through social media, byline editorials, speaking opportunities or other activities. The two should complement each other to enhance your business objectives and protect your brand.

While Identifying the differences between marketing strategies and other strategies, and seeing their importance and connection to each other and how they are mutually dependent to the success of each other, it is necessary that we implement he knowledge we have gained in knowing their differences and see to it that we identify the similarities and how well they work hand in hand.